A Sick History of
MEDICINE

NEON  SQUID

CONTENTS

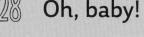
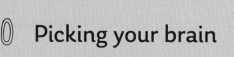

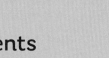

A SICK HISTORY OF MEDICINE

READ ON...IF YOU HAVE THE STOMACH FOR IT!

Humans have been fighting disease from the dawn of time. Over thousands of years, we've tried all sorts of medicines and operations to make us feel better. Some have changed and others have stayed the same. As you will see in the pages of this book, the history of medicine has been pretty gross!

WORM REMOVAL SERVICE

Some medical treatments haven't changed at all. Today, you can get ill from Guinea worm disease by drinking water infected with worm babies, or larvae. After a few years, the worms wriggle their way out through your skin. The only thing you can do is wrap the worm around a stick and tug it out, much like they did in the old days!

PLACES OF HEALING

Some of the oldest hospitals were called *bimaristans*. One of the earliest was built in Damascus, which is in modern-day Syria. Some hospitals only focused on one disease, such as leprosy, also known as Hansen's disease, which caused people a lot of trouble before we developed a cure.

FIRST SURGERY

In ancient India, doctors used the heads of ants and beetles to staple wounds shut! The surgeon would make sure the critter bit down and closed the cut.

You could probably use an ant in a "pinch" today, but doctors usually use special glue, staples, or threads to stitch you back up!

MEDICINE AND MAGIC

Throughout history, people believed that gods or evil spirits could make them ill. They would ask for help from healers who cast spells, performed magical rituals, and charmed jewelry for protection against sickness.

PAIN IN MY HEAD

If you had a pounding headache in ancient Egypt, a small clay crocodile was used to absorb your pain during healing rituals. Don't worry—it didn't bite!

Ancient Mesopotamian spirits such as Tiu loved to cause headaches. If you wanted to feel better, you had to smear a mixture containing goose fat all over your head.

The Kamayurá of Brazil believe a monkey spirit seeking revenge for its death causes headaches by smacking hunters on their heads.

WRITTEN IN THE STARS

Some people believe that the night sky might hold the secrets to our health. Doctors in medieval Europe (500 CE to 1500 CE) gazed at stars to pick the best time to perform surgery. Today, some healthcare workers worry that a full moon will bring chaos to a hospital!

DOUBLE, DOUBLE TOIL, AND TROUBLE

In 16th-century Scotland, people believed witches cackled and cast spells to make others ill. Some witches were just healers accused by patients unhappy with their treatment, and many were burned to death at the stake!

IN LATIN AMERICA, TRADITIONAL OR FAITH HEALERS CALLED *CURANDEROS* CAN OFFER PROTECTION FROM SPIRITS THOUGHT TO MAKE PEOPLE SICK.

FOREVER YOUNG

Do you want to live forever? You're not the only one. Some ancient Chinese emperors drank elixirs—drinks that were supposed to make them immortal. For the unlucky ones, the elixirs had the opposite effect and poisoned them! Elixir or not, all of the emperors eventually died.

ON THE MENU

Plants and foods have always been used to help people feel better. Ancient Greek doctor Hippocrates apparently came up with the saying "let thy food be thy medicine and medicine be thy food." He probably didn't think that people would take it as literally as they do!

THAT SHOULD DO THE TRICK...

LET IT RIP!

The ancient Greeks believed garlic could cause enough "wind" to blow away any blockages in your body that were making you feel icky.

DRINK ME IF YOU DON'T WANT YOUR TEETH TO FALL OUT.

SPARKLING AND GLOWING

Fizzy drinks such as tonic water were used to prevent malaria, a nasty illness caused by bites from infected mosquitoes. The main ingredient in tonic water is quinine, a herb used by the Quechua people of South America to treat chills and fevers. Quinine also glows in the dark! Try shaking tonic water and see for yourself.

HEALING TEA

When explorers started sailing around the world, they learned about medicine from different cultures. After traveling for months without fruits and vegetables, French explorer Jacques Cartier and his crew developed scurvy, which caused their teeth to fall out! When they finally arrived in North America, they learned from the native Haudenosaunee people that they could be cured with hot pine needle tea.

TIME FOR BREAKFAST

In the 1800s, people in the US worried that greasy foods such as bacon and eggs for breakfast caused stomachaches. Breakfast cereal was invented because it was easier to digest for sensitive stomachs.

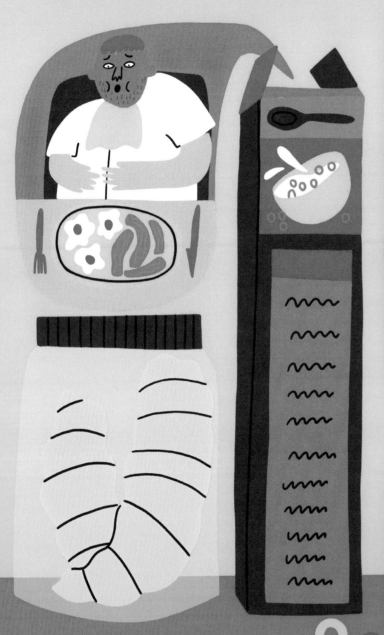

SECRETS OF THE SPICES

Spices such as turmeric were used to flavor food, color cosmetics, and even help you get over food poisoning. Today, turmeric can help calm sore and achy joints. It also happens to be super tasty in curries!

YE OLDE APOTHECARY

In the 19th century, you could take the time to make home remedies for whatever was ailing you, but it was easier to see your local healer, known as an apothecary, to buy medicines.

PLEASE HELP ME, WISE MAN. TELL ME YOU HAVE A PLAN.

They had a huge selection of medicines. Some were made from plants and herbs. Others, however...

I HAVE JUST THE THING FOR YOU.

MUMMY BRAIN

...could include ingredients such as ear wax, blood, mummy parts, and even poison!

ACHOO!

Why do we get sick? This is a question that healers have been asking themselves for centuries. Beyond bad luck or making a spirit angry, they worried whether people fell ill because of an imbalance of fluids in the body or stinky air that could spread disease.

A BALANCING ACT

Hippocrates came up with a theory where your health depended on the four humors or fluids that flowed around your body: black bile, yellow bile, blood, and phlegm. People believed that too much or too little of any one of these humors made you ill. To feel better, you would be given things to make you poop, throw up, or bleed...a lot.

SO MUCH FOR "JUST A PINCH"!

I DON'T THINK THIS IS WORKING.

GEORGE WASHINGTON

One day, American president George Washington came down with a sore throat. His doctors told him to gargle treacle and gave him pastes made from dried beetles. None of this helped, so they bled him to restore balance in his body. Bloodletting probably didn't kill him, but it also didn't help him feel any better!

DON'T COME ANY CLOSER!

THERE'S A STINK IN THE AIR

Health wasn't only based on the balance of your humors. People worried that poisonous, stinky air caused by waste and rotting bodies could spread disease. English nurse Florence Nightingale thought that deadly diseases, such as smallpox and cholera, were caused by air coming from the smelly drains flowing under the homes of many Londoners.

PEOPLE CARRIED SMALL CASES OF HERBS AND SPICES CALLED **POMANDERS** TO SNIFF TO KEEP THE BAD SMELLS AWAY.

YOU NEED A MASK

During plagues, such as the Black Death of the 14th century, doctors wore masks with long beaks stuffed with nice-smelling herbs to block out the bad smells and prevent them from falling ill.

SAFE AND STYLISH!

Pomander

CREEPY-CRAWLIES

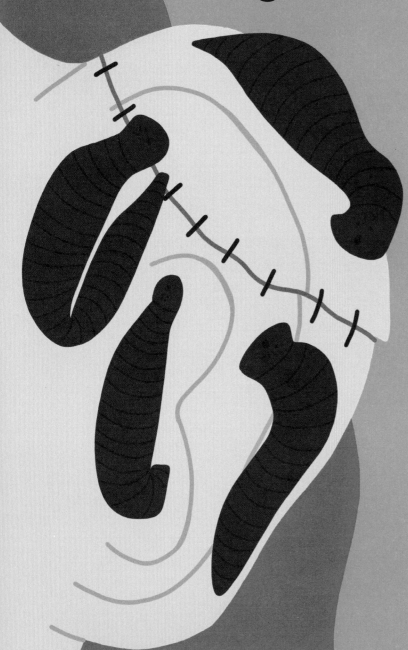

Hundreds of years ago, being sick meant that you could be treated with slimy little creatures, such as maggots and leeches. These creepy-crawlies are still used in treatments today! While some critters heal us, others like mosquitoes buzz around and bother us. Mosquitoes aren't just annoying—their bites can spread diseases you might have heard of before: malaria, dengue fever, Zika virus, and many more.

MAGGOTS

Surgeons serving in French emperor Napoleon's army noticed that maggots, or baby flies, saved the lives of soldiers wounded during battle. As gross as it was, wounds infested with maggots recovered quicker than those that weren't. This is because maggots are very skilled at eating dead skin, which cleans and heals cuts quickly.

LEECHES

Writings from ancient Egypt and India tell us that leeches are some of the oldest medical treatments around. Doctors use them to make blood flow better in tiny body parts sewn back together during surgery, such as the tips of our fingers and ears.

WE'RE GOING TO NEED BACK-UP.

The Maya of Central America also used maggots to treat wounds. The question is: How did the maggots get into the wound?

BEWARE THE MOSQUITOES!

The yellow fever virus got its name because it could make your skin and eyes turn golden. In the 1800s, Cuban doctor Carlos Finlay realized that a special kind of mosquito, *Aedes aegypti*, was causing yellow fever. These mosquitoes originally came from Africa and spread around the world on trade ships.

The Maya were clever—they wrapped bloody cloth around the infected limb to attract flies. These flies would lay eggs and...

...ta-da! Maggots hatched from the eggs. These hungry little creatures would then heal the cut.

THIS IS JUST WHAT I NEED!

SAVE YOUR PEE FOR A RAINY DAY

Some people claimed that Greeks and Romans mixed urine into their toothpaste to make their teeth shine bright. This is probably not true, but they might have used pee to get pesky stains out of their clothing! People also believed that drinking their own pee could make them feel better, live longer, or look even younger.

I SHOULD REALLY TRY EXERCISING INSTEAD.

DON'T HOLD YOUR NOSE

Back when people believed that sickness was caused by bad air, they cleansed their homes with flowers and spices. Others thought that fighting rotten air with even more foul odors was the best way to stay well. People kept smelly goats in their homes and spent time in the stinkiest places they could find. Often these were the town cesspits, which were holes where everyone dumped their poop!

BODY MEDICINE

Sometimes the best cure for when you're poorly comes from your own body... or another person's! Long ago, people thought that human flesh and blood had special healing powers. Pounding headache? Some powdered skulls made from ancient Egyptian mummies might help. Nasty nosebleed? A tasty jam made from human blood could replace some of the blood you lost. Many even turned to their own poop and pee to stay healthy!

THE POWER OF POOP

In ancient China, doctors served "yellow soup" to help patients with diarrhea and food poisoning. The main ingredient in this dish was sour poop! Nowadays, doctors still look to poop as a treatment by doing fecal transplants. They scoop up a healthy person's feces, or poop, and put it up the butt of a sick person. Germs in the healthy poop get rid of the bad bacteria that was making them feel icky.

GHASTLY GERMS

Tiny living things called microorganisms or germs can sneak into our bodies and make us ill. We didn't know that they existed for a very long time, probably because they were too small to be seen with our eyes. It wasn't until the 1700s that we realized that they were floating about and hurting us. How did we finally manage to spot and kill them?

TAKING A CLOSER LOOK

Dutch scientist Antonie van Leeuwenhoek was the first to spot germs through microscopes, which are powerful magnifying glasses.

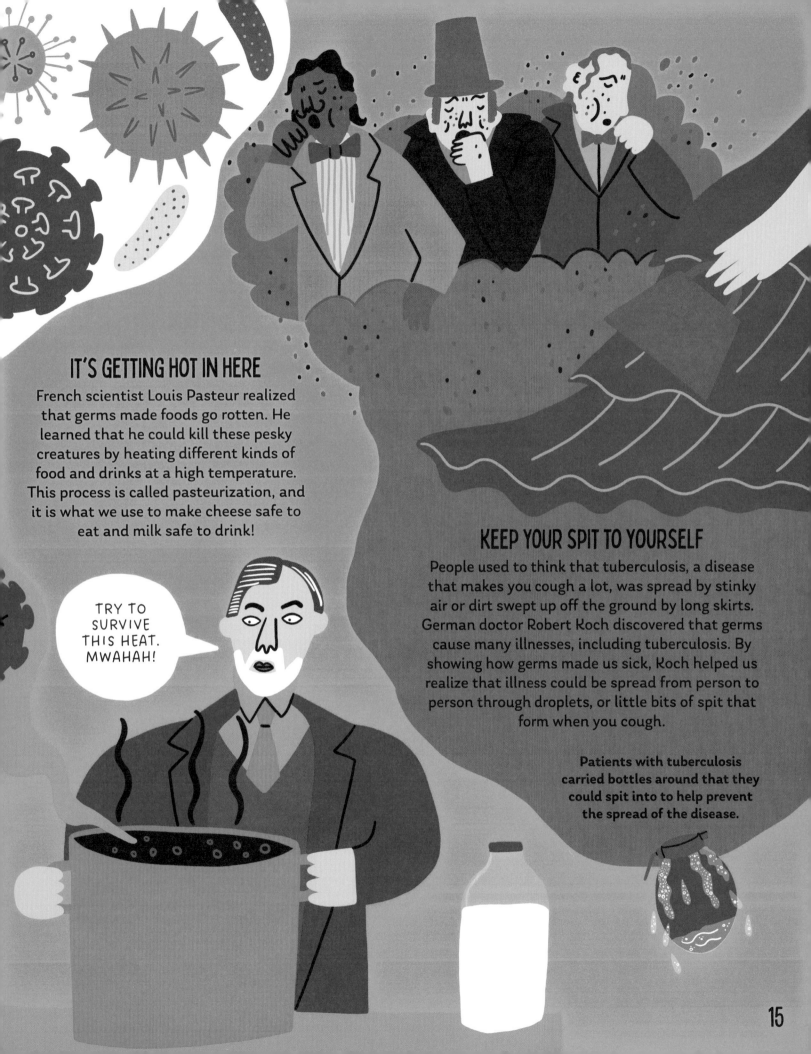

IT'S GETTING HOT IN HERE

French scientist Louis Pasteur realized that germs made foods go rotten. He learned that he could kill these pesky creatures by heating different kinds of food and drinks at a high temperature. This process is called pasteurization, and it is what we use to make cheese safe to eat and milk safe to drink!

TRY TO SURVIVE THIS HEAT. MWAHAH!

KEEP YOUR SPIT TO YOURSELF

People used to think that tuberculosis, a disease that makes you cough a lot, was spread by stinky air or dirt swept up off the ground by long skirts. German doctor Robert Koch discovered that germs cause many illnesses, including tuberculosis. By showing how germs made us sick, Koch helped us realize that illness could be spread from person to person through droplets, or little bits of spit that form when you cough.

Patients with tuberculosis carried bottles around that they could spit into to help prevent the spread of the disease.

PLAGUES

Epidemics are diseases that make lots of people very ill. They are sometimes called plagues and can be caused by germs like bacteria and viruses, which jump from person to person. Epidemics can also spread through infected bug bites or through animals such as pigs and cats. Plagues aren't always spread by germs—some might also be caused by the mind!

YOU'RE WELCOME.

THE BLACK DEATH

In the 1300s, fleas and ticks would bite humans and spread a terrible disease known as the dreaded "Black Death." It probably got this name because it caused the skin on your neck and armpits to swell up and turn black.

SPANISH FLU

Despite its name, the deadly Spanish flu of 1918 didn't start in Spain. It got its name because Spanish newspapers were the first to report this new illness. The flu probably started in the USA, and it killed over 20 million people worldwide.

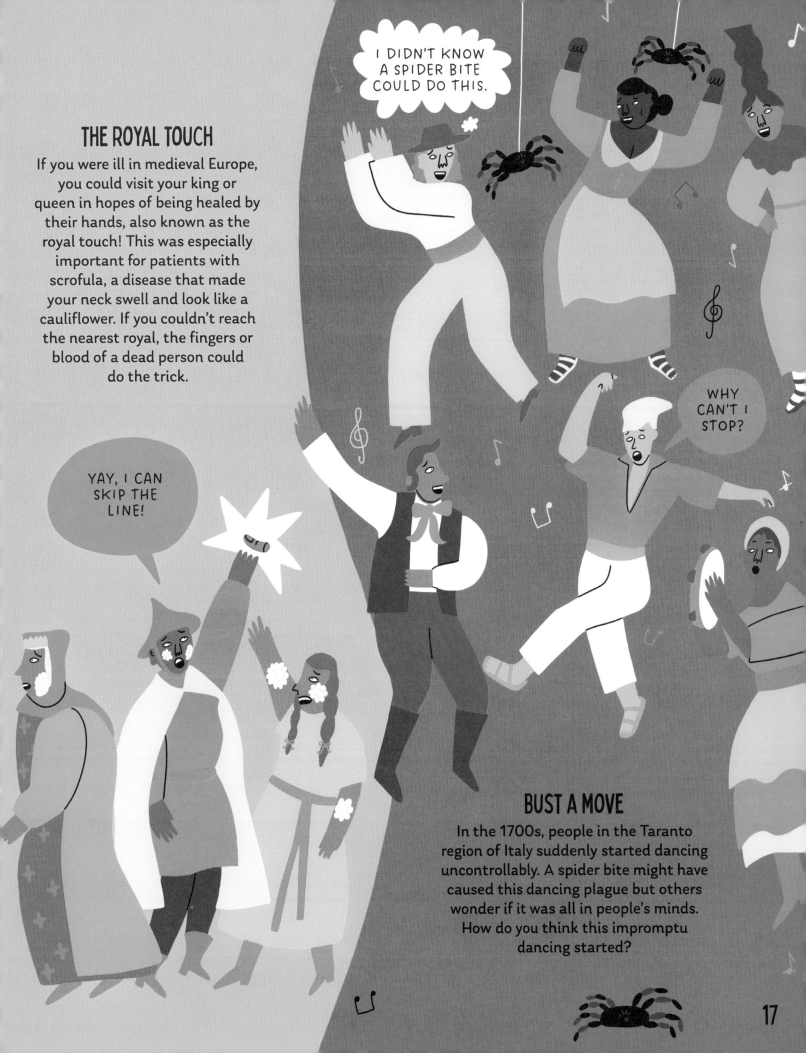

THE ROYAL TOUCH

If you were ill in medieval Europe, you could visit your king or queen in hopes of being healed by their hands, also known as the royal touch! This was especially important for patients with scrofula, a disease that made your neck swell and look like a cauliflower. If you couldn't reach the nearest royal, the fingers or blood of a dead person could do the trick.

BUST A MOVE

In the 1700s, people in the Taranto region of Italy suddenly started dancing uncontrollably. A spider bite might have caused this dancing plague but others wonder if it was all in people's minds. How do you think this impromptu dancing started?

TOO MUCH POOP!

THIRSTY?

Finding clean drinking water in 1800s London was hard. Many people drank water from the River Thames even though it had pieces of poop floating in it!

PUMP IT UP

English doctor John Snow realized people were getting sick from diseases that gave you terrible diarrhea such as cholera because they were drinking dirty water from the city pumps.

Keeping clean water and human poop separate hasn't always been easy, but it is important for our health. The Indus Valley Civilization used drains to flush away waste, while ancient Romans built special bridges called aqueducts to bring fresh water into their homes. However, about two hundred years ago, the city of London in England was fighting a losing battle against poop…

CAN SOMEONE HURRY UP AND INVENT AIR FRESHENERS ALREADY?!

THE GREAT STINK

One summer, the Thames was so smelly that it caused the "Great Stink of London." People were terrified by the smell because they worried sickness was spread by the stinky air. It wasn't until the smell affected Londoners' ability to work that politicians started thinking about building better sewers.

CESSPITS

As the number of people living in London grew, the cesspits holding their poop started to overflow into wells for clean drinking water. Workers called night soil men would wake up in the middle of the night to shovel the waste out of these pits.

TRY TO HOLD IT IN NEXT TIME, BUDDY.

THIS IS DISGUSTING EVEN BY MY STANDARDS.

VACCINES

To stop you from getting ill, scientists invented vaccines. With one quick poke, vaccines put bits of germs into your body to teach it to fight off the same germs if it ever meets them again. The first vaccine was created to fight off smallpox, a deadly disease that caused fevers and rashes.

Sweet flag

Shitala

> LAST SCAB, I PROMISE!

SMALLPOX-BUSTERS

Before vaccines were invented, people had different ways of treating smallpox. In Canada, the First Nations used the sweet flag plant to treat it. In India, people prayed to goddess Shitala for good health.

SNIFF THE SCABS

Infecting people with smallpox on purpose is called variolation. In the 1500s, Chinese doctors ground up the scabs of patients with smallpox and blew them up the noses of healthy people. This made the healthy people poorly with a much less dangerous form of smallpox. It protected them against future infection!

A HELPING HAND...OR LUNG

Before we had vaccine for a virus called polio, people would get so weak from it that they sometimes couldn't breathe on their own. They needed help from an iron lung, a long metal tube that was invented to breathe for them while they recovered.

Mirrors were attached to the iron lung machines to help patients see what was happening around them.

THE WORD "VACCINE" COMES FROM *VACCA*, THE LATIN WORD FOR COW. READ THE NEXT PAGE TO FIND OUT WHY...

HOW IT ALL STARTED

In the 1700s, English country doctors like Edward Jenner realized that people who got infected with cowpox, a disease spread from cows to humans, were less likely to get smallpox. Edward had an idea...

Edward collected pus from the sores on the hands of Sarah Nelmes, a dairy maid who was probably infected by the cows that she milked.

Edward rubbed the pus into cuts that he made on the arm of a young boy called James Phipps.

To test whether his idea had worked, Edward injected the boy with smallpox a few weeks later...

...and James didn't get sick at all. Vaccination against smallpox using cowpox worked!

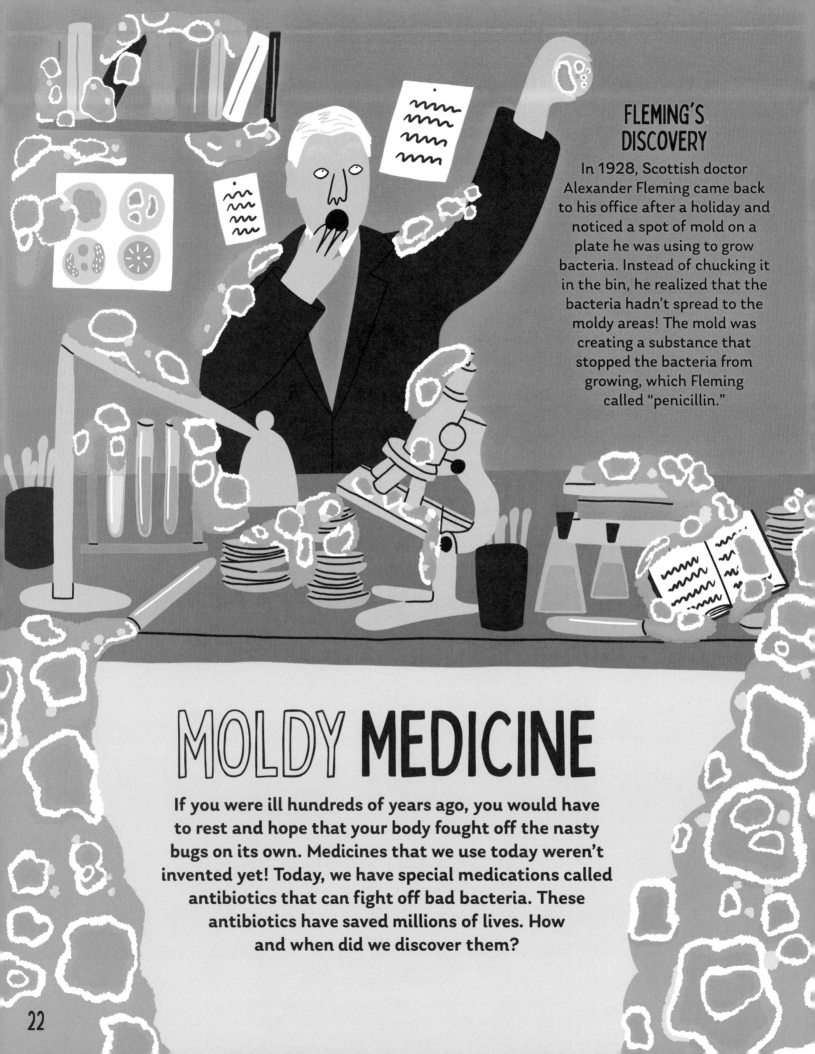

FLEMING'S DISCOVERY

In 1928, Scottish doctor Alexander Fleming came back to his office after a holiday and noticed a spot of mold on a plate he was using to grow bacteria. Instead of chucking it in the bin, he realized that the bacteria hadn't spread to the moldy areas! The mold was creating a substance that stopped the bacteria from growing, which Fleming called "penicillin."

MOLDY MEDICINE

If you were ill hundreds of years ago, you would have to rest and hope that your body fought off the nasty bugs on its own. Medicines that we use today weren't invented yet! Today, we have special medications called antibiotics that can fight off bad bacteria. These antibiotics have saved millions of lives. How and when did we discover them?

THE PENICILLIN GIRLS

Penicillin was special because it could fight off deadly bacteria. At first, it was very tricky to grow. Scientists at Oxford University in the UK used bedpans and cookie tins to grow the mold because they didn't have enough equipment! Many women scientists also helped produce penicillin. Some of them were even called the "penicillin girls."

A FRUITFUL DISCOVERY

Producing enough penicillin to treat patients during World War II was a real challenge. A scientist known as "Moldy Mary" found a new, faster growing mold on a rotting melon. She cut the moldy bits off and shared the rest of the melon with her team. Do you think it was tasty?

GERM-FIGHTER

Penicillin was not the first medicine that attacked germs. A medicine called Salvarsan was discovered by Japanese scientist Sahachiro Hata and German scientist Paul Ehrlich. It treated an infection called syphilis. It was also safer than mercury, a poison that was the only other treatment for syphilis at that time.

WHO GOT THERE FIRST?

People have been using mold to kill bacteria for a long time! In ancient China, people would scrape mold off beans, cheese, or bread to treat infections. Costa Rican scientist Clodomiro Picado Twight may have even discovered penicillin before Fleming, but he is best known for his work on snake antivenom.

SECRETS OF THE BODY

The human body is a mystery. To understand how it worked, doctors cut into, or dissected, dead bodies to reveal its secrets. Learning from human and animal bodies helped them understand how the body keeps us alive! They learned how the heart pumps, recycles, and moves blood around the body...but they also got in trouble for what they did.

IT LOOKS LIKE A BIG WORM.

SO THAT'S WHAT BOWELS ARE!

I HAVE A GREAT VIEW.

PUBLIC DISSECTIONS

After doing dissections in secret for many years, people realized that medical students needed to learn how to slice bodies open if they were going to be good doctors and surgeons. Italian surgeon and anatomist Andreas Vesalius started to host public dissections, which eventually turned into parties! People wore masks and costumes, and even danced to music as the dissection was performed.

READY FOR THE AFTERLIFE

In ancient Egypt, dead bodies were carefully prepared for the afterlife. Organs were pulled from the body and saved in special canopic jars. Embalmers—the people preparing the body—were some of the first people to see the brain, which they pulled out through the nose!

DISSECTION WAS BANNED IN MANY COUNTRIES AND CULTURES THROUGHOUT HISTORY.

Canopic jars

GRAVE ROBBERS

A few hundred years ago, medical schools had a hard time finding fresh bodies for dissection. This created a grave-robbing business. In the middle of the night, robbers would sneak into graveyards, dig up bodies, sneak them out, and sell them to medical schools!

TODAY, PEOPLE DONATE THEIR BODIES TO MEDICAL SCHOOLS FOR STUDENTS TO LEARN FROM AFTER THEY HAVE DIED.

HEY! THAT'S MY UNCLE DAVE.

I'M GOING TO POKE YOUR BRAIN IF YOU DON'T HOLD STILL!

Medicine that you swallow or rub onto your skin isn't always enough to heal you. You might need an operation or surgery, where doctors called surgeons use special tools to work on or inside your body. Surgeries have been performed for thousands of years. Many surgeries have been helpful, while others were dangerous. Some were painless, but others would be very painful!

READY, SET, AMPUTATE

To save your life, sometimes you would need to lose an arm or a leg in a surgery called an amputation. English surgeon Robert Liston competed with other doctors to see how quickly he could amputate a limb. His record is under three minutes! Back then there wasn't medicine that was good at taking pain away or putting patients to sleep, so working quickly meant that the patient didn't suffer for too long.

TREPANATION

One of the oldest surgical procedures is called trepanation, or having a hole drilled in your skull. This was a treatment for head injuries, such as a broken skull or even headaches! It has been used by many cultures, such as the Kisii in Kenya. In medieval Europe, doctors thought that cutting the head open could help patients with mental illnesses.

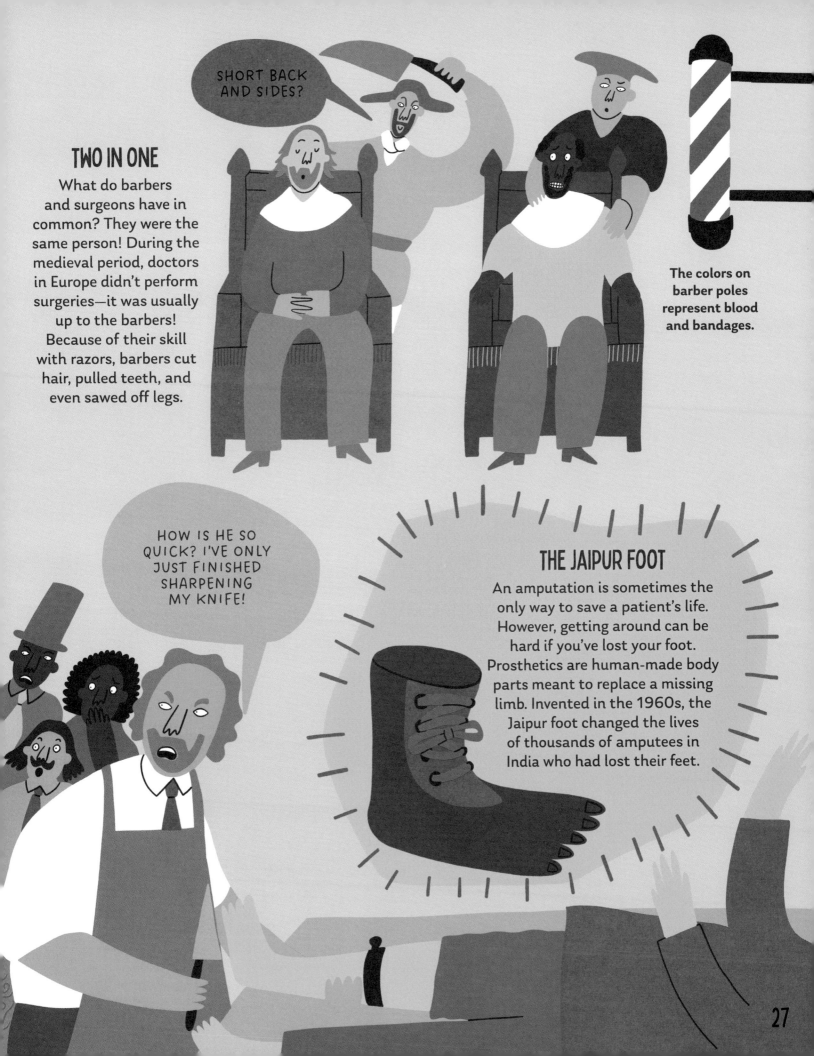

TWO IN ONE

What do barbers and surgeons have in common? They were the same person! During the medieval period, doctors in Europe didn't perform surgeries—it was usually up to the barbers! Because of their skill with razors, barbers cut hair, pulled teeth, and even sawed off legs.

SHORT BACK AND SIDES?

The colors on barber poles represent blood and bandages.

HOW IS HE SO QUICK? I'VE ONLY JUST FINISHED SHARPENING MY KNIFE!

THE JAIPUR FOOT

An amputation is sometimes the only way to save a patient's life. However, getting around can be hard if you've lost your foot. Prosthetics are human-made body parts meant to replace a missing limb. Invented in the 1960s, the Jaipur foot changed the lives of thousands of amputees in India who had lost their feet.

OH, BABY!

Having a baby is a tale as old as time. For thousands of years, healers called midwives have helped moms have their babies. Today, doctors and scientists have developed tools to make childbirth as safe as possible, but in the past it wasn't always easy, and it could be very dangerous!

TODAY, TOOLS SUCH AS FORCEPS AND SUCTION DEVICES CAN BE USED TO HELP PULL A BABY'S HEAD OUT.

I THINK I'D RATHER NOT...

CAUGHT IN A SPIN

People have dreamt up bizarre ways to make childbirth easier. American engineer George Blonsky and his wife Charlotte imagined a machine where moms would be strapped to a table and then spun at high speeds to push the baby out! The goal was for the baby to fly out and be caught in a net... hopefully. Thankfully this machine was never used in real life. Some things might be better left as ideas.

WASH YOUR HANDS

Hungarian doctor Ignaz Semmelweis wanted to stop moms and babies from dying during childbirth. He realized this was happening because doctors weren't washing their hands after cutting up dead bodies, so their dirty hands would infect the moms with deadly germs.

MAYBE GIVE THEM ANOTHER SCRUB.

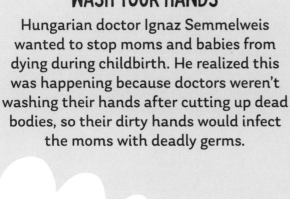

FEARFUL IMPRESSIONS

People used to believe that a mother's fear could affect her baby's appearance. One story says that a pregnant woman saw a mouse jump out of a flour tin. It scared her so badly that her baby was born with a suspiciously mousy birthmark!

FLOUR

PICKING YOUR BRAIN

Our brains are like the engines of our bodies—they make us who we are! They help us think, feel, and act. Scientists and doctors have spent a long time studying the brain to understand it better, but it still holds many mysteries.

IT'S JUST A SCRATCH

In 1848, a man named Phineas Gage was helping build railroads when a metal rod went into his head, through his brain, and out the other side! Amazingly, he survived! However, people soon noticed that his personality had changed, and he was acting strangely. His accident helped us understand that different parts of the brain control different parts of our body and behavior.

CRIMINAL MINDS

In the 19th century, doctors tried to predict a person's personality by feeling the lumps and bumps on their head! This was called phrenology. They even made masks of dead criminals to try to understand why they did bad things. We now know that this was bad science, or pseudoscience.

YOU'RE NEXT, DOC.

TALK TO ME

Brains can get sick in different ways. One of these is called mental illness. It can make people feel sad, scared, or confused. Today, doctors may give patients medicine or talk to them to help them feel better. Doctors like Anna Freud, daughter of famous psychoanalyst Sigmund Freud, pioneered talk therapy, where patients speak with therapists to feel better.

UH-OH! GOOD FOR THE ANTS, BAD FOR MY PATIENT.

THE ART OF EXAMINATION

We don't always need to be cut open for doctors to understand why we are ill. Some of a doctor's most important tools are their eyes, ears, noses, and hands. Healers throughout history have used senses such as hearing, taste, and smell to figure out why someone was feeling poorly.

PEE HOLDS THE ANSWER

Doctors used to look at, smell, and even taste pee to figure out what was wrong with their patients! Healers used "pee wheels" to compare the color of your pee and judge your health. Ancient Indian doctors such as Sushruta realized that sweet and sticky pee attracted black ants. This was a sign of a disease we now call diabetes.

Some people thought they could predict your future from a pee wheel!

ON TAP

As the son of an innkeeper, doctor Leopold Auenbrugger might have watched workers tap barrels of beer or wine to see how full or empty they were. His childhood probably inspired him to tap on the chests of patients to understand how the heart and lungs sound.

LISTENING IN

French doctor René Laënnec discovered that a long paper tube could help him listen to a heart more clearly. He invented a wooden tube called a stethoscope to help doctors hear the heartbeats.

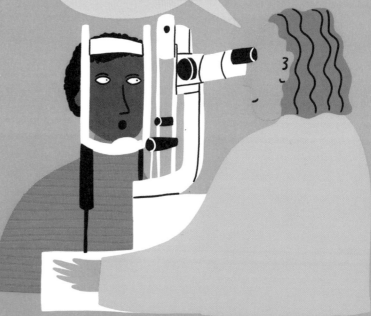

CAN YOU READ THE FIRST LETTER FOR ME?

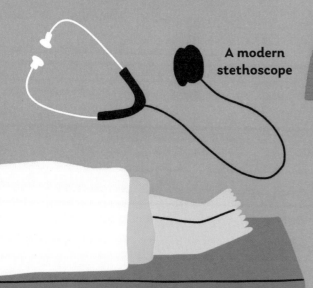

A modern stethoscope

MODERN TECHNOLOGY

Today, doctors, dentists, and eye doctors have even more tools to help them see why patients are sick. One of these tools is the ophthalmoscope, which lets them look into someone's eyes. Doctors can also attach tiny cameras to other "scopes" to look down our throats, or even into our bellies!

X-RAY VISION

How can we look inside the human body? Doctors could do that through surgery, but that's painful and messy. What if they could take a picture to show you what was wrong without needing to cut you open? This is what X-rays do. They help us to see why someone is ill or if they've broken a bone!

I HAVE SEEN MY DEATH!

SEEING INSIDE

In 1895, German scientist Wilhelm Röntgen learned that a special ray of radiation could pass through solid materials, such as the human body. He figured out a way to take a picture of these rays and called these photographs "X-rays." One of the first X-rays was of William's wife's hand. Apparently she wasn't too happy about it!

MARIA SKŁODOWSKA-CURIE

Scientist Maria Skłodowska-Curie, or Marie Curie, was the first woman to win a Nobel Prize. She discovered two radioactive elements, called radium and polonium. During World War I, she developed ambulances called "petit Curies," which helped doctors on the battlefields X-ray injured soldiers.

STICK YOUR FOOT IN HERE, SIR

X-rays weren't always used for medical reasons. Some shoe shops purchased X-ray machines to measure the shoe size of their customers! Today, we use other machines in addition to X-rays to take pictures of the body, such as CAT and PET scans. Sadly, no pets are involved!

BECAUSE MARIE CURIE WASN'T PROTECTED WHILE DOING HER WORK, AFTER SHE DIED SHE WAS BURIED IN A LEAD COFFIN TO PREVENT THE RADIATION IN HER BODY FROM HURTING OTHERS.

RADIUM THERAPY

In the early 1900s, people believed that radium was healthy for you. They started putting it in everything, from water to make-up. One American businessman, Eben Byers, drank so much radium water for his health that his jaw fell off! Today, radium is found in some kinds of radiation therapy, which is a special treatment used to kill off cancer cells.

WHAT A SHOCK!

People have always been energized by electricity. After the electric battery was created, people put on shows where they shocked the human body and showed off how it sparked. Electricity was also seen as a miracle treatment for disease. Its jolts could help you, zap you painfully, and, in some cases, do nothing for your health.

ANCIENT SHOCKS

The ancient Egyptians, Romans, and Greeks used electric animals such as catfish, eels, and stingrays to treat pain, headaches, and even baldness! To cure yourself, they suggested rubbing the fish on your feet.

FANCY A BATH?

Have you heard of the electric bath? Some baths needed you to sit in water while a gentle electrical current passed through your body. Not all of them needed water, and you would just be "bathed" in the current instead! These baths were supposed to make sore joints and tummies feel better but probably weren't very helpful.

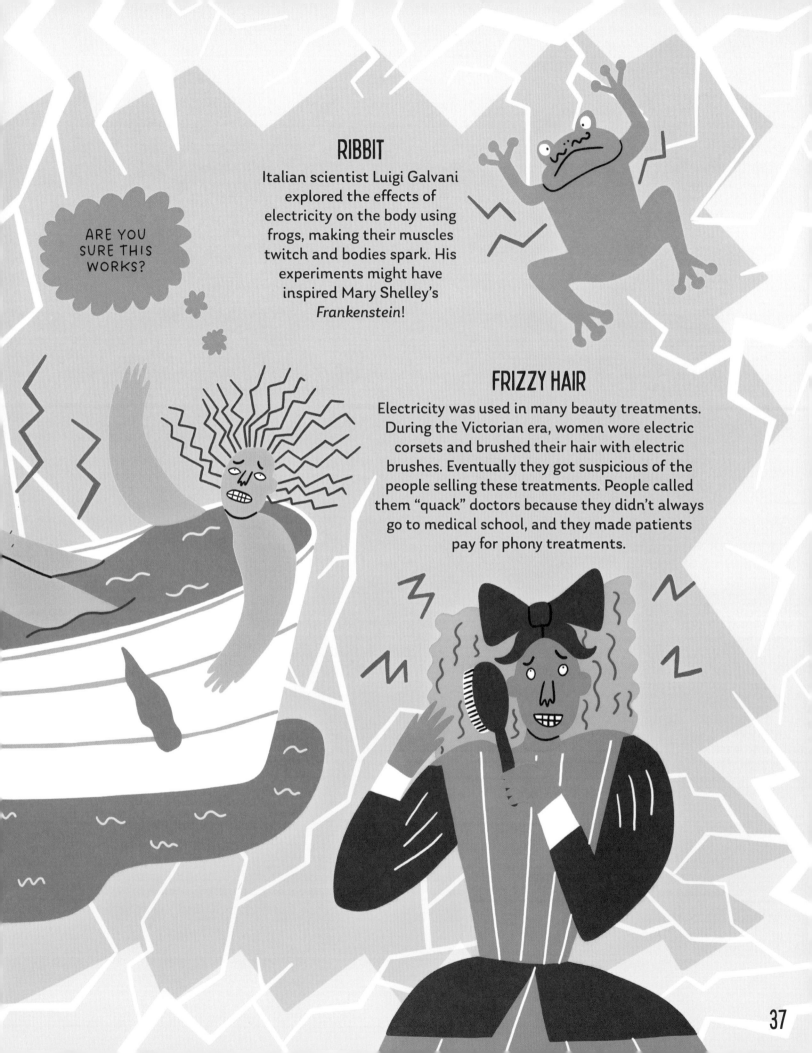

RIBBIT

Italian scientist Luigi Galvani explored the effects of electricity on the body using frogs, making their muscles twitch and bodies spark. His experiments might have inspired Mary Shelley's *Frankenstein*!

FRIZZY HAIR

Electricity was used in many beauty treatments. During the Victorian era, women wore electric corsets and brushed their hair with electric brushes. Eventually they got suspicious of the people selling these treatments. People called them "quack" doctors because they didn't always go to medical school, and they made patients pay for phony treatments.

ARE YOU SURE THIS WORKS?

A TRIP TO THE DENTIST

Having strong, healthy teeth is important. Without them, you would have a pretty hard time chewing your food! People have straightened and pulled teeth for thousands of years to make themselves look and feel better, but they haven't always known why teeth rot or how to fix them without pain.

ROUTINE VISIT

Today, you can go to the dentist when you have a toothache or for a checkup. In the past, you could go to a barber (who cuts your hair) or a blacksmith (who works with metal) to get your teeth pulled.

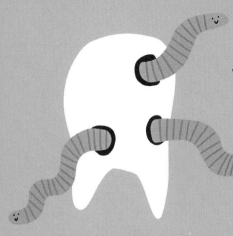

TOOTH WORMS

How do teeth rot? People used to believe that tooth worms lived in teeth, ate away at them, and created small holes called cavities.

LAUGHING GAS

People used nitrous oxide, also known as laughing gas, to host what must have been some hilarious parties. By testing the gas on themselves, scientists realized that it could numb pain, which would be useful when pulling teeth. Since then, dentists have invented more ways to take away our pain to make sure we are comfortable when being treated.

MIGHT AS WELL PULL OUT ANOTHER! HAHA!

EMBRACE THE BRACES

Wanting straight teeth is not a new trend. Gold bands wrapped around teeth have been found on ancient Egyptian mummies, though they were probably put there after the people had already died. Queen Marie Antoinette wore braces to straighten her crooked teeth before she moved from Austria to the glamorous French court.

EXPLODING TEETH

In the 1800s, a man had such bad tooth pain that he buried his head in the ground! The next morning, the tooth exploded with a loud noise, like a pistol shot, and he felt much better. We're still not sure why this happened, but don't worry, it's very rare!

BECOMING A DOCTOR

What does it take to become a doctor? Thousands of years ago, students of medicine read books, attended lectures, and worked alongside other doctors to learn the art of medicine, much like they do today! Like their ancestors, modern doctors also go through busy, sleepless nights to learn how to treat patients.

A RISKY BUSINESS

Being a doctor wasn't always easy, and it could even cost you your life. According to a set of Babylonian rules called Hammurabi's Code, doctors could lose their fingers—and their lives—if they killed a patient in surgery.

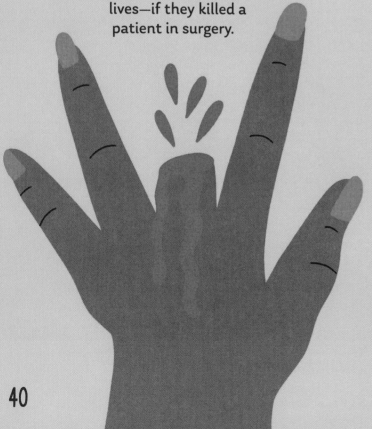

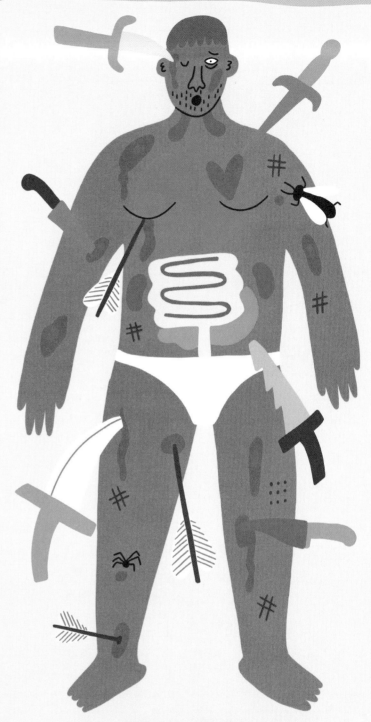

THE WOUND MAN

If you were working alone and were confused about how to treat your patient in the 15th century, there were special human body maps, such as the Wound Man, that could guide you. These maps told you how to treat anything from simple cuts and spider bites to injuries your patient got in battle, such as sword wounds and arrows stuck in their body!

EAGER TO LEARN

In the medieval period, students studied texts by famous doctors and scholars such as doctor and philosopher Ibn Sina. They also performed dissections on pigs and monkeys to learn about the human body because it wasn't always easy—or allowed—to find a human body to dissect.

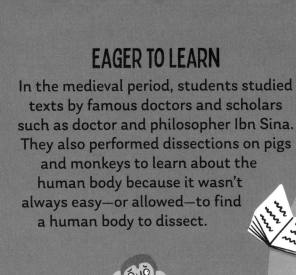
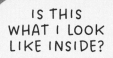

SCHOOL'S IN

In the 1300s, medical schools across the world started to be created. One of the first was in Salerno, Italy. This school admitted women, such as gynecologist Trota of Salerno, who wrote books on women's health and disease. She also treated "wind in the womb," which sounds like a painful stomachache.

TAKE THE OATH

In ancient societies, medical students watched and worked with doctors before they could see patients on their own. The students would swear an oath, like the Hippocratic Oath, to treat patients. Today, depending on where you are in the world, students still take a version of this oath!

People who have transformed medicine are known as pioneers. Many of them were scientists, surgeons, nurses, and midwives, as well as other healers. Their lives weren't always easy, especially if they were a woman. Depending on where they were born, what they looked like, who they loved, and how much money they had, they weren't always allowed to work and, if they did, their work was sometimes stolen! Let's recognize some of the trailblazers who made modern medicine what it is today.

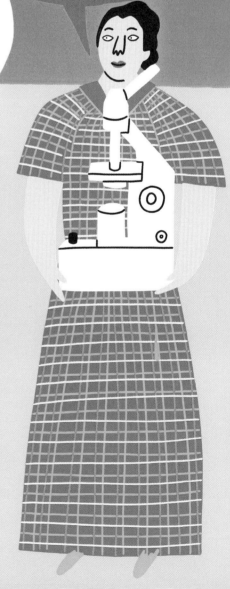

42

I'm doctor Sophia Jex-Blake. Along with six friends, I fought for women to be allowed to go to medical school in the United Kingdom.

I'm Tu Youyou. I received the Nobel Prize for finding a cure for malaria. My research shows that the sweet wormwood plant can treat high fevers caused by the illness.

WHOSE IDEA WAS THIS?

BAKE ME A CAKE

In the medieval period, German healer Hildegard of Bingen used cloves to treat "stuffiness of the head" or even the dreaded hiccups! She also suggested that cakes made out of mole's blood, duck's beak, and goose feet could help some people feel better.

PROSTHETIC TOE

Some of the world's earliest healers come from ancient Egypt. One of the world's first female doctors was called Peseshet. She trained midwives and may have performed surgeries such as amputations. A notable surgery from 3,000 years ago involved a wooden prosthetic toe made for the daughter of a priest. It was meant to look nice and help her walk without tripping!

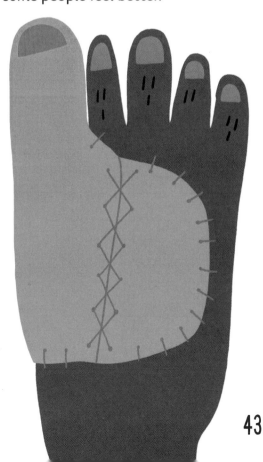

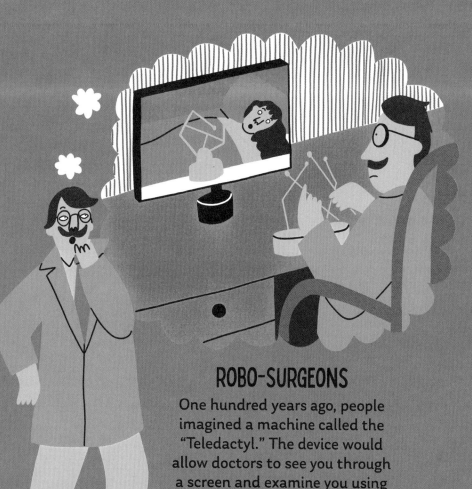

WHAT'S NEXT?

Have you wondered what medicine will look like in the future? So did the people who came before you! In the 1960s, people wondered whether an "instrument suit" could be invented, which would send your medical information to doctors to help them diagnose you. Do we have something like this today? Let's discover some other inventions that people have imagined and see which ones became reality.

ROBO-SURGEONS

One hundred years ago, people imagined a machine called the "Teledactyl." The device would allow doctors to see you through a screen and examine you using spindly arms that they remote-controlled from their office. Something similar exists today! Surgeons can operate on patients hundreds of miles away thanks to remote-controlled robotic arms.

HEAD TRANSPLANTS

Some of the first successfully transplanted organs between humans were kidneys, which means that a kidney was taken from one person and sewn into another. Today, we can transplant livers, lungs, intestines, and hearts. Do you think we could transplant heads one day?

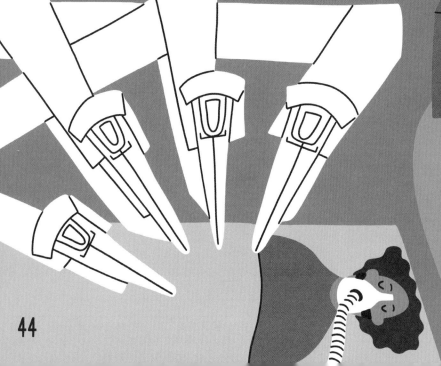

OUT OF THIS WORLD

As we explore more of space, we need to think about how to do operations in zero gravity. Surgery on your tummy would be hard because your guts move differently in space. Your intestines and blood droplets would float around. Imagine the mess!

I'VE TAKEN GRAVITY FOR GRANTED...

TAKE YOUR PICK!

CLONES

Dolly the sheep was one of the first animals to be cloned—she was an exact replica of another sheep! She was born using a technique that could potentially be used to bring extinct animals back to life. Scientists hope that cloning human cells could one day help us treat diseases.

GLOSSARY

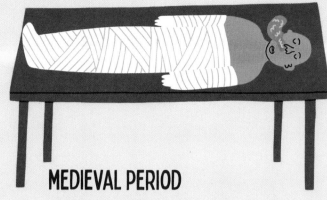

ANTIBIOTIC
Medicine that fights off bacteria that cause infections.

BACTERIA
Tiny living things, or microorganisms, that can help us stay healthy but can also make us sick.

BLOODLETTING
Taking blood out of a person's body to try to make them feel better.

CESSPIT
A hole in the ground where waste, such as poop, is buried.

CHOLERA
A bacterial infection of the tummy that causes very runny poop.

DOCTOR
Someone who practices medicine and helps heal sick people.

EMBALMER
Someone who preserves the bodies of people who have died.

EPIDEMIC
A disease that spreads quickly and makes a lot of people very ill.

GYNECOLOGIST
A doctor who specializes in the female reproductive organs.

MEDIEVAL PERIOD
A period of European history between the years 500 CE and 1500 CE. Also known as the Middle Ages.

MOLD
A kind of fungus that is used in medicine. Mold also grows on cheese, bread, and fruit.

PHRENOLOGY
The study of the lumps, bumps, and size of a person's head.

PSYCHOANALYST
A person who treats mental health conditions by talking to patients.

STETHOSCOPE
A tool that doctors and nurses put on your chest to listen to your heart.

SURGEON
A doctor who is trained to do operations, or surgeries.

TRANSPLANT
Moving a healthy organ, such as a heart, from one body to another to replace an organ that isn't working well.

X-RAY
Energy waves that are used to take a picture of your insides.

INDEX

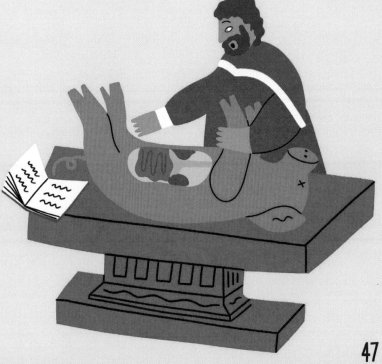

This has been a

NEON 🦑 SQUID

production

To all curious minds.

Author: Dr. Jelena Poleksic
Illustrator: Ella Kasperowicz

Editor: Malu Rocha
US Editor: Jill Freshney
Proofreader: Joseph Barnes
Indexer: Elizabeth Wise

Created for St. Martin's Press
by Neon Squid
The Smithson, 6 Briset Street,
London, EC1M 5NR

EU representative: Macmillan
Publishers Ireland Ltd,
1st Floor, The Liffey Trust Centre,
117–126 Sheriff Street Upper,
Dublin 1, D01 YC43

10 9 8 7 6 5 4 3 2 1

Library of Congress Cataloging-in-
Publication Data is available.

Printed and bound in Guangdong,
China by Leo Paper Products Ltd.

ISBN: 978-1-684-49449-1

Published in March 2025.

www.neonsquidbooks.com